SEA GIANTS OF DINOSAUR TIMES

BY 'DINO' DON LESSEM

ILLUSTRATIONS BY JOHN BINDON

LERNER BOOKS • LONDON • NEW YORK • MINNEAPOLIS

To Brian Joseph, my first friend, who has nothing whatsoever to do with anything in this book

First published in the United Kingdom in 2009 by
Lerner Books,
Dalton House,
60 Windsor Avenue,
London SW19 2RR

Website address: www.lernerbooks.co.uk

This edition was updated and edited for UK publication by Discovery Books Ltd.,
First Floor, 2 College Street, Ludlow, Shropshire SY8 1AN

Words in **bold type** are explained in the glossary on page 32.

British Library Cataloguing in Publication Data

Lessem, Don
  Sea giants of dinosaur times. - 2nd ed. - (Meet the
  dinosaurs)
  1. Marine reptiles, Fossil - Juvenile literature
  I. Title
  567.9'37

ISBN-13: 978 0 7613 4343 1

Printed in Singapore

TABLE OF CONTENTS

MEET THE SEA GIANTS 4

WATER WONDERS 6

LIFE IN THE SEA 12

WHAT HAPPENED TO THE SEA GIANTS? . . . 26

GLOSSARY 32

INDEX 32

MEET THE SEA GIANTS

WELCOME, DINOSAUR FANS!
I'm 'Dino' Don. I LOVE dinosaurs. I also love the other weird animals that lived during dinosaur times. When dinosaurs ruled the land, giant reptiles ruled the seas. Come and meet these amazing ocean animals. You won't even need to get your feet wet!

ARCHELON
Length: 3.5 metres
Home: western North America
Time: 70 million years ago

ICHTHYOSAURUS
Length: 1.8 metres
Home: western Europe, North America
Time: 180 million years ago

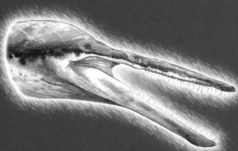

KRONOSAURUS
Length: 13 metres
Home: north-eastern Australia
Time: 120 million years ago

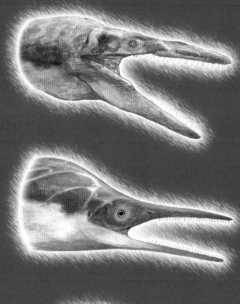

MOSASAURUS
Length: 14 metres
Home: North America
Time: 65 million years ago

OPTHALMOSAURUS
Length: 3.4 metres
Home: western Europe, North and South America
Time: 150 million years ago

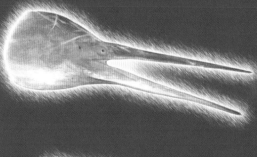

PLESIOSAURUS
Length: 2.4 metres
Home: western Europe
Time: 180 million years ago

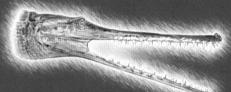

SHONISAURUS
Length: 15 metres
Home: western North America
Time: 220 million years ago

TELEOSAURUS
Length: 3 metres
Home: western Europe
Time: 180 million years ago

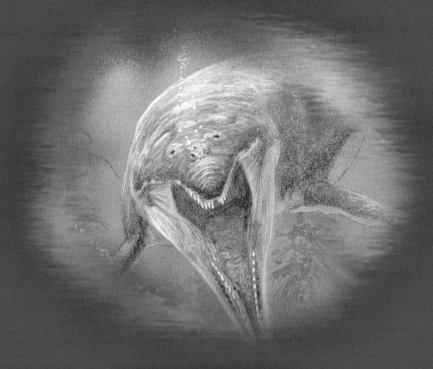

WATER WONDERS

We are deep under water 120 million years ago. Two huge *Kronosaurus* fight over a large fish. Each *Kronosaurus* is as long as an ice cream van. Snap! One *Kronosaurus* grabs the fish with its sharp-toothed jaws.

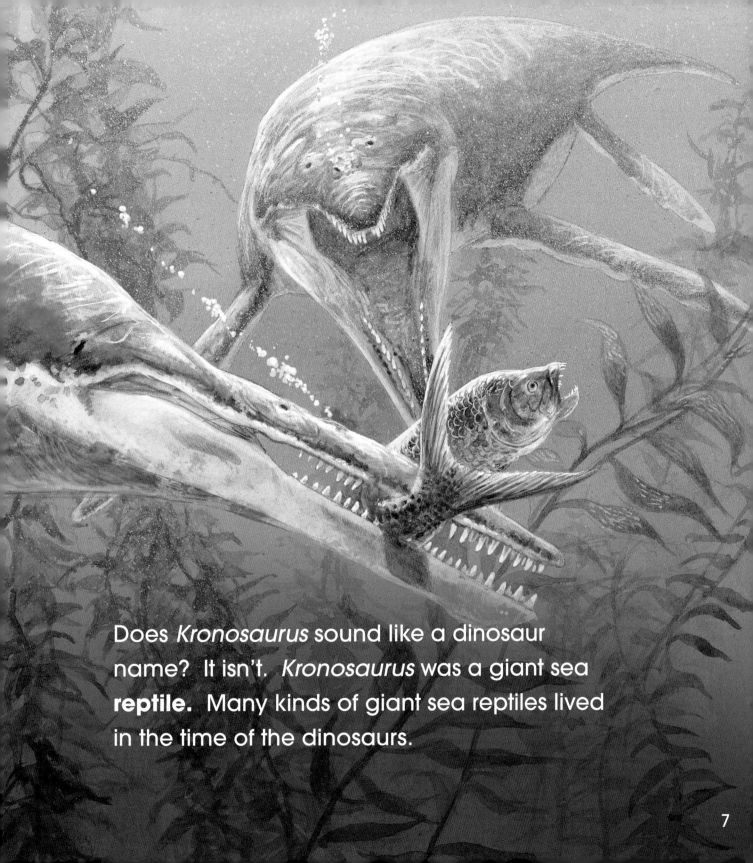

Does *Kronosaurus* sound like a dinosaur name? It isn't. *Kronosaurus* was a giant sea **reptile.** Many kinds of giant sea reptiles lived in the time of the dinosaurs.

THE TIME OF THE SEA GIANTS

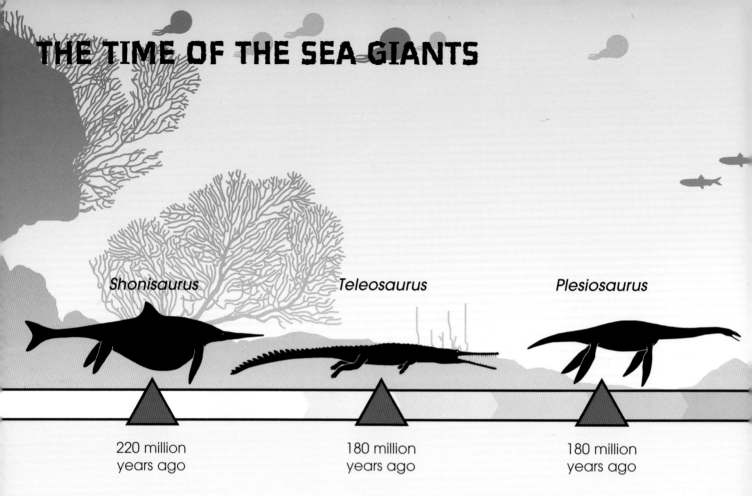

Shonisaurus   Teleosaurus   Plesiosaurus

220 million
years ago

180 million
years ago

180 million
years ago

Giant sea reptiles were not dinosaurs.
Dinosaurs came into the water to swim. Sea
reptiles lived in the water. Dinosaurs had arms
and legs, but most sea reptiles had flippers.
Baby dinosaurs hatched from eggs. At least
some kinds of sea reptiles were born live.

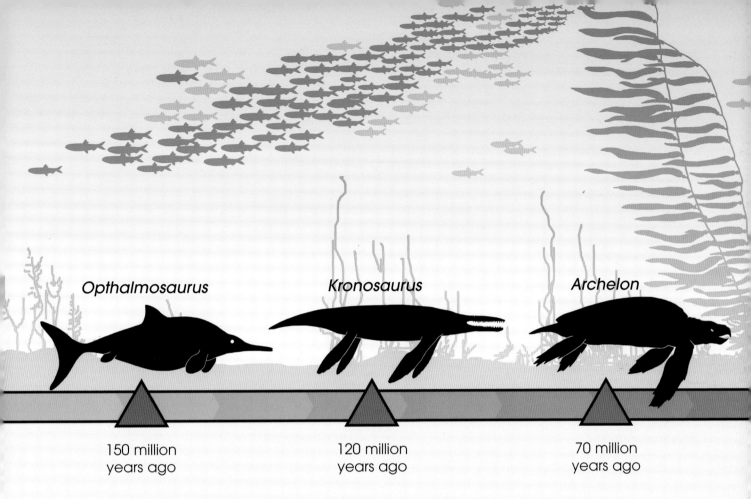

Opthalmosaurus

Kronosaurus

Archelon

150 million
years ago

120 million
years ago

70 million
years ago

Like all reptiles, the sea giants had scaly skin.
All sea reptiles breathed air with their lungs.
However, there were many different kinds of sea
reptiles. Some were **predators** that hunted fish.
Others ate eggs. Some were shaped like
dolphins. Other sea reptiles had long necks
and bodies. Still others had short, thick bodies.

SEA GIANT FOSSIL FINDS

The numbers on the map on page 11 show some of the places where people have found fossils of the giant sea reptiles in this book. You can match each number on the map to the name and picture of the sea reptiles on this page.

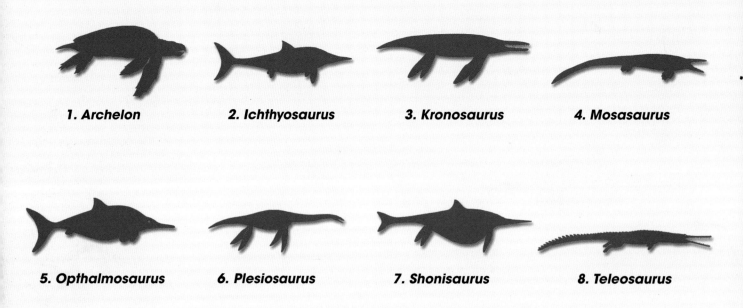

1. Archelon   **2. Ichthyosaurus**   **3. Kronosaurus**   **4. Mosasaurus**

5. Opthalmosaurus   **6. Plesiosaurus**   **7. Shonisaurus**   **8. Teleosaurus**

How do we know about the sea giants? For hundreds of years, people have found and studied the traces sea reptiles left behind when they died. **Fossils** of bones, eggs and teeth have shown us how the giants looked and lived. So far, we've discovered hundreds of giant sea reptiles.

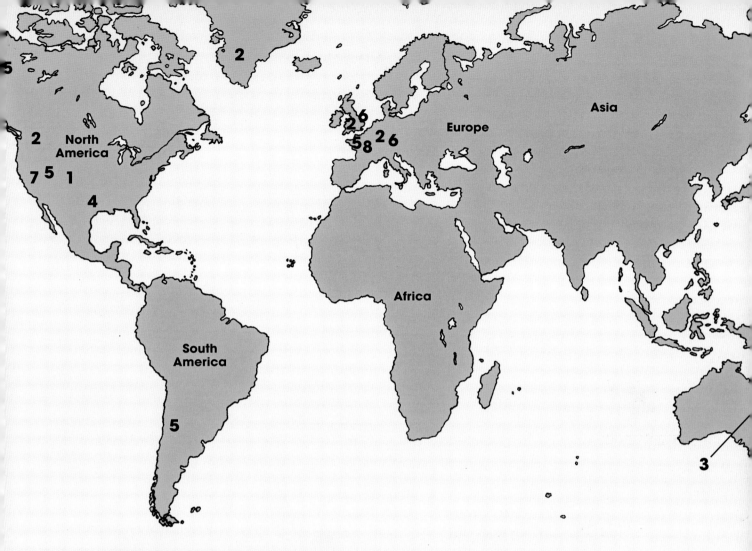

Giant sea reptiles lived in the world's oceans. So why does this map show sea reptiles on land? Some places were under water during sea giant times. Scientists have found fossils in those places. It is too hard to look for fossils at the bottom of the sea!

LIFE IN THE SEA

How did the sea giants survive in the ocean? Finding enough food wasn't easy for such large animals. However, they had many different ways of hunting.

The sea grows dark late in the day.
Opthalmosaurus chooses this time to hunt.
With its big eyes, this giant sea reptile can
see well in dark water. The fish it chases
don't see it coming – until it's too late.

Archelon uses huge flippers to move itself quickly through the water. It attacks a group of jellyfish. The jaws of *Archelon* are not strong. Its beak has no teeth. The soft jellyfish are a perfect food for this giant.

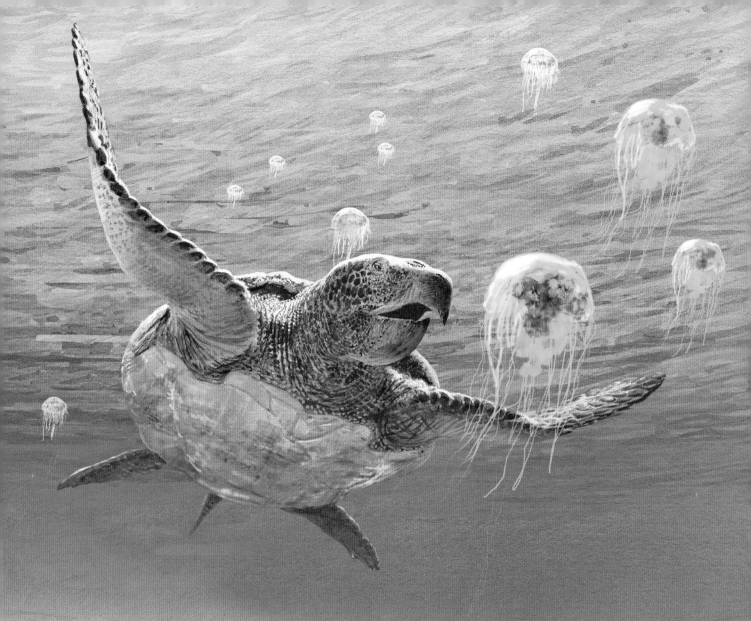

Archelon was the largest turtle of dinosaur times. It didn't have the heavy shell of the turtles we know. Instead, its shell was made of bony ribs that were covered with rubbery skin.

Teleosaurus swishes quickly through the
water. Its short legs are tucked up against
its body. It is as long as a large rowing boat.
This sea crocodile closes in on a squid.
Teleosaurus snaps up the squid with long,
narrow jaws full of pointy teeth.

Since before the time of the dinosaurs, crocodiles have lived in rivers and swamps around the world. In dinosaur times, some crocodiles grew to be longer than buses. Some, like *Teleosaurus,* swam out in the deep ocean.

Mosasaurus opens its powerful jaws. It is hunting a slow ammonite. The ammonite's thick shell can't protect it against *Mosasaurus*. The sea giant crushes the shellfish with its sharp, cone-shaped teeth.

18

Mosasaurus was one of the biggest and deadliest sea giants of all. This ocean hunter sometimes grew to be more than 14 metres long. That's longer than a *Tyrannosaurus rex!*

Plesiosaurus searches for groups of fish to eat. This sea giant could use its long neck to reach out and grab fish. Then *Plesiosaurus* might have dived to the seabed to swallow stones.

Why did it eat stones? The stones tumbled around in the sea reptile's stomach. They helped to grind up the fish that *Plesiosaurus* ate. Perhaps they also added weight to help *Plesiosaurus* swim under the water for longer.

A group of *Shonisaurus* called a **pod** swims through the water. The pod surrounds a school of fish. Working together, the huge sea reptiles herd the fish and eat them.

Shonisaurus was one of the biggest of all sea reptiles. Its body was longer than half a tennis court! Scientists think that *Shonisaurus* may have lived in pods, like dolphins. However, it didn't swim the way that dolphins do. *Shonisaurus* moved its tail from side to side. Dolphins flap their tails up and down.

Fossils show us how some sea reptiles were born. This photo shows a small baby flowing out from under the tail of a dolphin-like sea reptile. *Ichthyosaurus* is giving birth! The baby swims freely from the moment it is born. It searches for small ocean creatures to eat.

An adult *Ichthyosaurus* was much smaller than
Shonisaurus. The tiny babies of *Ichthyosaurus*
could not protect themselves. Two or three
were born at one time. That way, at least one
might escape becoming dinner for a hungry
predator.

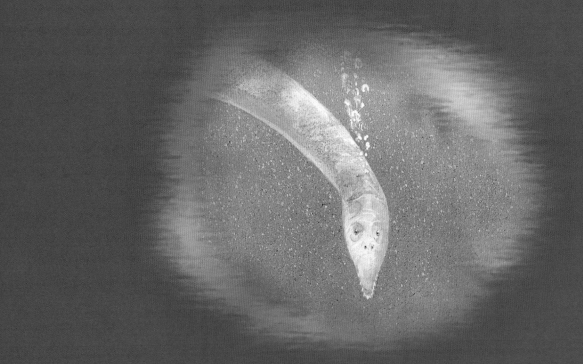

WHAT HAPPENED TO THE SEA GIANTS?

The great sea reptiles disappeared 65 million years ago. The last of the dinosaurs died out then too. What killed them? Many scientists think that changes in the Earth's weather made it hard for huge animals to find food.

The British coast is one of the best places to find fossils of sea giants. Fossils have taught us many things about how the giant sea reptiles lived. We've even learned from fossilized poo! It shows that *Ichthyosaurus* ate fish.

Most fossils are not found by scientists. Nearly 200 years ago, a boy named Joseph Anning found a strange skull in the cliffs near his home in the south of England. A year later, his 12 year old sister Mary found the rest of the skeleton. It was the first known *Ichthyosaurus*!

This photo shows Mary's *Ichthyosaurus* discovery. This skeleton wasn't her only great discovery. She also found a *Plesiosaurus* and many other fossils. Mary's amazing finds created great interest in **palaeontology,** the science of studying ancient life.

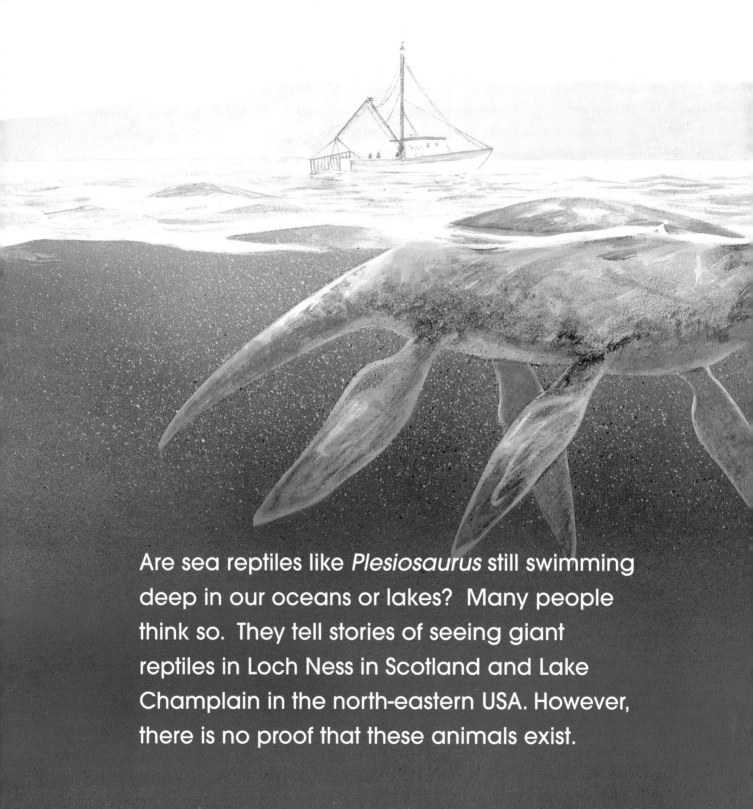

Are sea reptiles like *Plesiosaurus* still swimming deep in our oceans or lakes? Many people think so. They tell stories of seeing giant reptiles in Loch Ness in Scotland and Lake Champlain in the north-eastern USA. However, there is no proof that these animals exist.

Large animals may live deep in the Earth's waters. But they are not living plesiosaurs. Sea reptiles died out 65 million years ago. They can never come back. We can only imagine how amazing they were.

GLOSSARY

fossils: the remains, tracks or traces of something that lived long ago

palaeontology: the study of ancient living things from their fossils

pod: a small group of animals that swim and eat together

predators: animals that hunt and eat other animals

reptile: an animal that has scaly skin and breathes air with its lungs

INDEX

birth 8, 24–25

dinosaurs 7–8, 26

eyes 13

flippers 8, 14

fossils 10-11, 24, 27-29

hunting 6, 9, 12-14, 16, 18-19, 20, 22, 24

pods 22-23

skin 9, 15

teeth 6, 10, 14, 16, 18

Text copyright © 2005 by Dino Don, Inc.
Illustrations copyright © 2005 by John Bindon
First published in the United States of America in 2005
The photographs in this book appear courtesy of: © The National
History Museum, London, pp 24, 27, 28–29.